LIFE
Dogs
Why We Need Them. Why They Need Us.
MW01629263
JOHN DOMINIS/LIFE/THE PICTURE COLLECTION

# Contents



I-IMAGES/EYEVINE/REDUX

# Dogs


EDITORIAL DIRECTOR Kostya Kennedy
EDITOR Courtney Mifsud
DIRECTOR OF PHOTOGRAPHY Christina Lieberman
DESIGNER Sharon Okamoto
COPY CHIEF Parlan McGaw
COPY EDITOR Joel Van Liew
PICTURE EDITOR Rachel Hatch
WRITER-REPORTER Ryan Hatch
PHOTO ASSISTANT Alessandra Bianco
PRODUCTION Richard Shaffer

**TIME INC. BOOKS, A DIVISION OF MEREDITH CORPORATION**
PUBLISHER Margot Schupf
SENIOR VICE PRESIDENT, FINANCE Anthony Palumbo
VICE PRESIDENT, MARKETING Jeremy Biloon
EXECUTIVE DIRECTOR, MARKETING SERVICES Carol Pittard
DIRECTOR, BRAND MARKETING Jean Kennedy
SALES DIRECTOR Christi Crowley
ASSOCIATE DIRECTOR, BRAND MARKETING Bryan Christian
ASSOCIATE DIRECTOR, FINANCE Jill Earyes
ASSISTANT GENERAL COUNSEL Andrew Goldberg
SENIOR MANAGER, FINANCE Ashley Petrasovic
SENIOR BRAND MANAGER Katherine Barnet
PREPRESS MANAGER Alex Voznesenskiy
ASSOCIATE PROJECT AND PRODUCTION MANAGER Anna Riego Muñiz

EDITORIAL DIRECTOR Kostya Kennedy
CREATIVE DIRECTOR Gary Stewart
DIRECTOR OF PHOTOGRAPHY Christina Lieberman
EDITORIAL OPERATIONS DIRECTOR Jamie Roth Major
MANAGER, EDITORIAL OPERATIONS Gina Scauzillo

SPECIAL THANKS Brad Beatson, Brett Finkelstein, Melissa Frankenberry, Kristina Jutzi, Simon Keeble, Seniqua Koger, Kate Roncinske





Published by LIFE BOOKS, an imprint of Time Inc. Books, a division of Meredith Corporation • 225 Liberty Street New York, NY 10281





Vol. 18, No. 9 • April 27, 2018




We welcome your comments and suggestions about LIFE Books. Please write to us at:
LIFE Books, Attention: Book Editors
P.O. Box 62310, Tampa, FL 33662-2310

For more one-of-a-kind LIFE special editions and keepsakes, go to LIFEspecialeditions.com.

**FRONT COVER:** GLOBALP/ISTOCKPHOTO/GETTY

# Dogs

BY KOSTYA KENNEDY

AMERICA IS HOME TO ABOUT 90 MILLION dogs, a sometimes quiet, invariably curious, and often rollicking mass of canines who have the essentials of life never far from mind: Love, food, fun, sleep. If there's one thing about dogs, they know how to live. It's not quite true that dogs rule the planet—though, as the *Seinfeld* bit has it, an alien observer might draw that conclusion after watching humans bending to dutifully scoop up dog droppings. But it does sometimes seem that a pup's outlook on existence, in its simplicity of wants and its simplicity of virtues (loyalty chief among them, empathy too), represents a life-form that has things figured out.

There are exceptions. Dogs can be like humans. Some dogs are nuts. Some are skittish, or inappropriately exuberant, or lazy. They can be given to possessiveness and envy. The German expression *Salat Hund,* which means salad dog, refers to the dog, who, despite his ancient-bred carnivorousness, would eat even a bowl of lettuce and tomatoes should he think that the dog beside him wants to eat it too.

They sit when you say "Sit!" and come when you call "Come!" and raise their front paw to shake your hand, just because they know you like it. These are animals who can drive a herd or guard a home or nose out a felon in hiding. And yet the things they will do for our amusement! Skateboarding, skydiving, dancing on their hind legs. They balance things on their snouts and wear women's clothes. Where would *America's Funniest Home Videos* be without them? Dogs do what they are told and they also do what they want. Hence the after-bath shake, the rolling in unspeakable mud, the Halloween candy that suddenly disappears.

We blanket a clan that encompasses hundreds of breeds, from affenpinscher to Yorkshire terrier. The world's largest dog (Great Dane) is 40 times the size of the smallest (Chihuahua). The breeds have their traits and we celebrate them as only humans can, chronicling the instincts of Buck, the sled dog, in *The Call of the Wild;* and the courage of Old Yeller, a black mouth cur; and the fellowship of the Jack Russell terrier in *My Dog Skip.* In terms of integrity it's not the breed that matters. It's the doghood. Benji is a mutt.

As a rule, dogs and books go well together. John Grogan's dog memoir *Marley & Me* has sold more than 5 million copies. W. Bruce Cameron's *A Dog's Purpose* spent 49 weeks on the best-seller list. In fact, for people given to the pleasures of books and reading—and if you are here, you are among them—a book may be the dog's strongest rival as a companion for humankind. As Groucho put it: "Outside of a dog, a book is man's best friend. Inside of a dog it's too dark to read." ■

While most dogs have brown eyes, some breeds like Siberian huskies and border collies can have eyes with striking blue hues.

**Sun and Surf**
Golden retrievers are consistently one of the most popular breeds in America. Their love of play makes them a great match for kids.

GALLERY

# It's a Dog's Life

## A testimony to the running, splashing, soaring canine spirit

WU XIAOLING/XINHUA/EYEVINE/REDUX

AMY SANCETTA/REX/SHUTTERSTOCK

**Interoffice Romance?**
Brutus (the big fella) and Midge work together in the K-9 unit of the Geauga County, Ohio, sheriff's office.

**Once Around the Park and Home, James**

Pecorino, right, the adopted pup of landscape photographer Toni Anzenberger, and a taxi driver on the island of Capri, Italy.

TONI ANZENBERGER/ANZENBERGER/REDUX

LUKA DAKSKOBLER/XINHUA/EYEVINE/REDUX

**Taking the Plunge**

**On September 10, 2016, the town of Kamnik, Slovenia, hosted its second Flying Dogs dock-diving competition, in which athletic pups competed for titles and cash prizes based on length of jump.**

**Forever Friends**
**The love of a pet dog is a powerful aid for children trying to cope with stress and has an overall benefit on a child's emotional health and well-being.**

PETER DENNEN/AURORA

MATHIAS AHRENS/AURORA

## A Fetching Pair

**Young or old, big or small: Frequent physical activity is important to keeping a dog happy and healthy. These Australian shepherds in Germany stay on the move.**

**Fire Department Friend**

Twenty, the mascot of the New York City Fire Department's Ladder 20 Fire Station, was a gift from two Rochester, New York, sheriffs after the World Trade Center attacks. The dalmatian helped rebuild morale.

MARIO TAMA/GETTY

"It's just the most amazing thing to love a dog, isn't it? It makes our relationships with people seem as boring as a bowl of oatmeal."
—John Grogan, *Marley and Me*

TOM NEBBIA

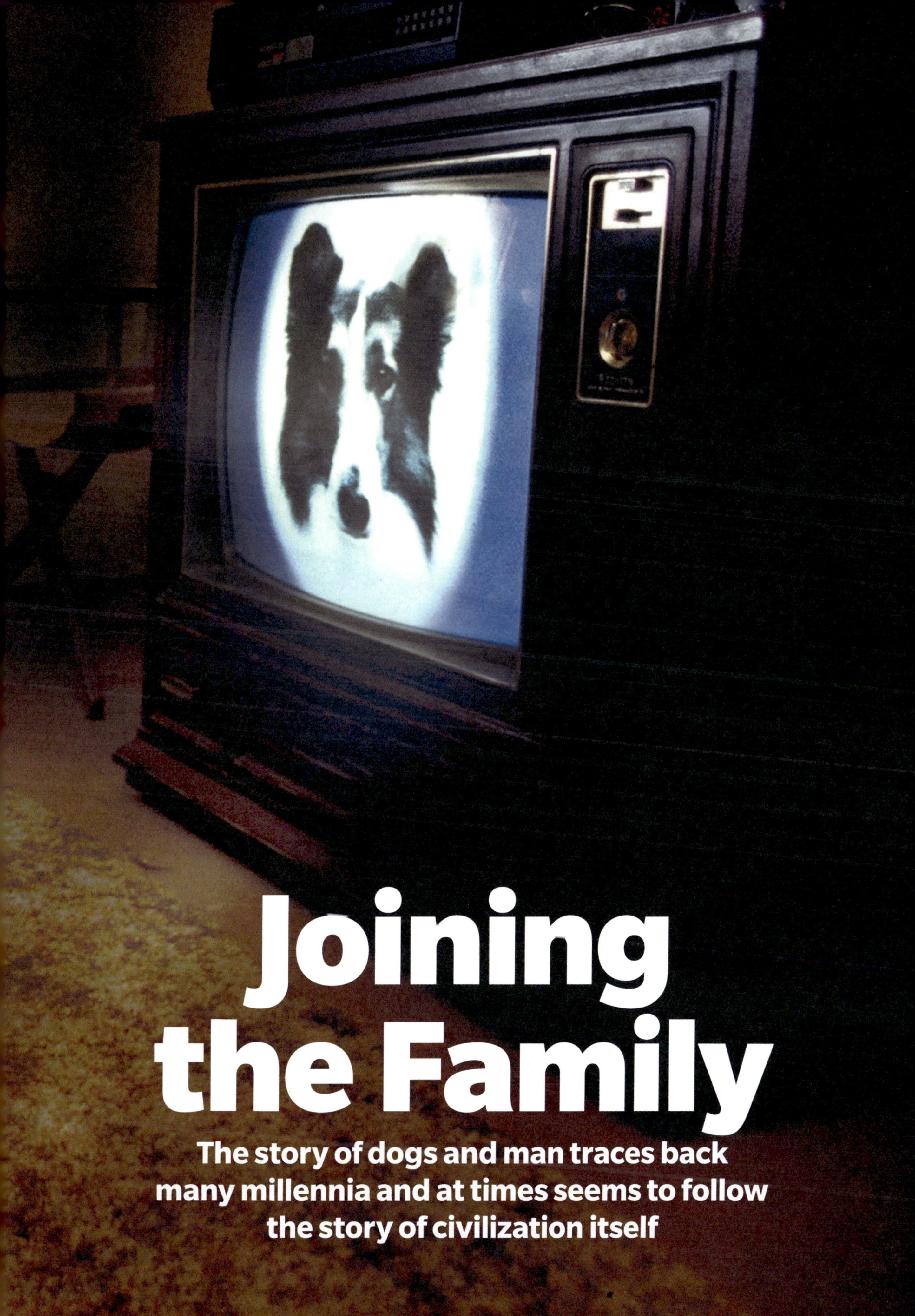

# Joining the Family

**The story of dogs and man traces back many millennia and at times seems to follow the story of civilization itself**

# Dancing with Wolves

## Dogs aren't just part of human civilization, they've helped us become more civilized

BY COURTNEY MIFSUD

In 1774, Lord John Murray Dunmore had a lot on his mind. As the new governor of Virginia, he had just championed the opening of the western lands and led a military attack against the Shawnee Indians, and he was awaiting the arrival of his family, who were en route from Scotland. He had also lost his dog. Glasgow, a brown-and-white bulldog known for snoozing and growling behind the walls of the Governor's Palace in Williamsburg, seemed to have been stolen from the grounds. Lord Dunmore promptly advertised a reward in the *Virginia Gazette,* offering 20 shillings (more than a month's wages for a farmer) for Glasgow's safe return. Dunmore's concern for his pet reflects the shifting view of dogs throughout history. The early days of the republic were at hand, but it was a lost dog that occupied the governor's attention.

Dogs were the first animals to be domesticated, making them our earliest pets. But nailing down exactly when we started living with "man's best friend" is tricky.

Researchers agree that dogs descended from wild wolves, but where and when the separation occurred is a point of disagreement. A 2016 study determined that dogs originated from two distinct wolf populations, one located in Europe and another in Asia. That meant that there were two distinct periods of domestication, both about 20,000 years ago, with the two lineages subsequently combining to become modern dogs.

But a July 2017 DNA study changed the conversation. After tracing the rate of mutations in dog genomes, the study found that dogs actually diverged from wolves roughly 40,000 years ago, all at once instead of in separate waves. According to this study, the split between European and Asian groups occurred about 20,000 years after the initial domestication event. What will it take for scientists to settle the debate? "More ancient dog DNA from genomes will ultimately solve the problem," says Krishna Veeramah, an author of the 2017 study.

We may not have nailed down the when, but we do have an idea on the

ART MEDIA/PRINT COLLECTOR/HULTON/GETTY

The future King Charles II with his siblings, and a mastiff, in this 1637 Van Dyck oil painting. The portrait's subject was a true dog lover: The King Charles spaniel is named for him.

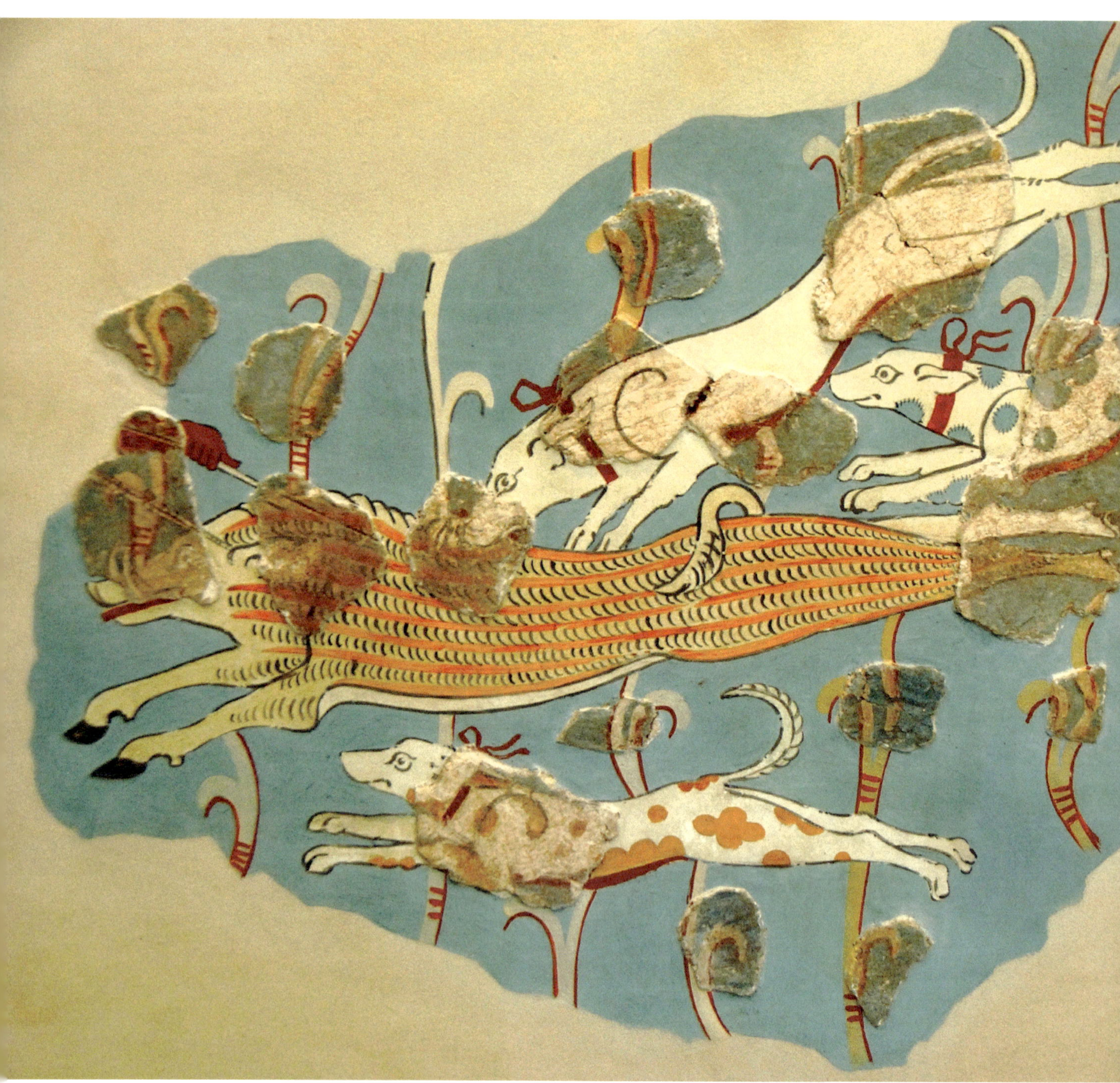

why. It's not that humans domesticated dogs, but rather that dogs changed themselves to adapt to us. According to Veeramah, the process began when wolves that would usually have to hunt on their own started to encroach on hunter-gatherer camps to scavenge for leftover food, taking advantage of the resources humans had to offer. "Those wolves that were tamer and less aggressive would have been more successful at this," Veeramah explained. "While the humans did not initially gain any kind of benefit from this process, over time they would have developed some kind of symbiotic relationship with these animals."

By 7,000 years ago, domesticated dogs were the norm, although they were not what we would consider pets. According to Veeramah, they resembled what we today know as village dogs, semisocialized and semiwild canines that breed freely and do not reside in people's homes. Modern breeds of dogs came later, when humans bred them as herders or hunters.

DOGS AND HUMANS BEGAN TO TRUST each other as a means to survive, but when did we begin to bond with our canine companions? In roughly 10,000 BCE in Ain Mallaha in northern Israel, two beings were buried together in the same grave: a woman and a four-month-old puppy, her hand gently resting upon the dog. This is the first evidence we have of a special bond

PRISMA/UIG/GETTY (2)

Much of what we know about man's earliest relationships with dogs, we have learned from art. Above, hounds are depicted hunting a wild boar in a Greek fresco dated between the 14th and 13th centuries BCE. Right: This wall painting from the tomb of the pharaoh Thutmose IV, circa 1400 BCE, shows the jackal-headed Anubis, god of the dead. In ancient Egypt, jackals were often seen in cemeteries.

between humans and dogs.

Ancient Egyptians are known for their love of cats, but they made a place for dogs. Like other ancient civilizations, Egyptians found dogs useful as hunters, but they also saw them as companions. A cave painting from 3500 BCE illustrates a scene that looks like it could be out of modern day: a man walking his dog on a leash. There's evidence that the Sumerians, who resided in Neolithic Mesopotamia, developed early versions of the leash and the dog collar.

With the advent of the Common Era, this bond became more and more evident. Chinese emperor Ling Ti of the Han dynasty (168–190 CE) admired his dogs so much that he fed them the finest foods, assigned them special bodyguards, and gave them ranks of great importance. Romans in the same period kept small dogs as pets, and their deaths were felt as keenly as one might feel that of a child. A dog's tombstone in Rome circa 200 CE reads, "To Helena, foster child, soul without comparison, and deserving of praise." Another reads, "I am in tears, while carrying you to your last resting place, as much as I rejoiced when bringing you home in my own hands 15 years ago."

During the Middle Ages in Europe, hunting shifted from a necessary survival struggle to a sport of the nobility. On the hunt, lords would hang back from the action as their servants searched for deer in the forest. When a deer was spotted, a horn would blare, and a dozen or more hounds would race through the brush as the hunting party followed. These specially bred and trained dogs were treated like nobility—above the common cur—and, as partners in the hunt, attained an elevated status. These hounds were addressed as "sir" or "my friend." They had their paws soaked in a tub after a hunt and slept in beds sometimes more comfortable than the servants'.

Hunting hounds weren't the only dogs who received special treatment in the Middle Ages. Monarchs bred their favorite types of dogs. Throughout 16th-, 17th-, and 18th-century art, toy spaniels are depicted in portraits and scenes of the nobility. These small dogs, with flat heads and pointed noses, were popular with noble ladies, and they were a particular favorite of King Charles II of England, who

ANN RONAN PICTURES/PRINT COLLECTOR/GETTY

reigned during much of the late 17th century. According to legend, he decreed that his beloved pups would be allowed into any public space, including the houses of Parliament. The breed is known today as the King Charles spaniel.

From the mid 1600s to the mid 1800s, Japan's rulers kept the island nation isolated, practically closed off from the rest of the world. During this time, in 1680, Tsunayoshi Tokugawa became shogun, the military ruler of Japan. Tokugawa presided over a vibrant period that saw a flourishing of the arts, academics, and agriculture, and he left a lasting legacy in protecting animals. The shogun issued a series of penal codes on animal protection called the Orders on Compassion for Living Things, which functioned as early animal welfare laws. Tokugawa particularly favored dogs (he was born in the Year of the Dog). He punished owners if their dogs were injured, and his government built kennels in Edo to house and protect stray dogs.

Some of these laws veered into the eccentric. One man who deserted his sick horse was forced into exile on a remote island, and in some cases residents were forcibly evicted from their homes to make room for these kennel facilities. Tokugawa's successor abandoned these orders, but in a world where no official animal protection laws were in place, 17th-century Japan had them on the books.

**Medieval hunting hounds, like those in the 15th-century scene above, were cherished companions. The screen panel opposite shows the appreciation of dogs in 17th-century Japan.**

DEAGOSTINI/GETTY

VINTAGE IMAGES/GETTY

MARY EVANS

In the late 19th century, dogs that once ran wild shared in the comforts of hearth and home. Children, like the Victorian-era girl opposite, learned to care for and train their new friends. Dogs were also essential playmates, as seen above at the turn of the 20th century.

GOVERNOR DUNMORE'S REGARD FOR his dog Glasgow was not an exception in 18th-century Colonial times. Canines were claiming more and more of man's affection. Benjamin Franklin once wrote, "There are three faithful friends—an old wife, an old dog, and ready money." There were countless lost-dog ads like the one for Glasgow: A general's Pomeranian named Spado fetched a hefty $20 reward in 1777—that's more than $400 today.

It wasn't until the 19th century that the Western world started to catch up to Japan's regulations for humane treatment of animals. In 1822, Irishman Richard Martin lobbied in the United Kingdom for legislation outlawing cruelty to animals. His efforts were successful, and two years later he helped shape the world's first animal welfare organization, the Royal Society for the Prevention of Cruelty to Animals. This elevated appreciation for animals clashed with some traditional religious notions. David Grimm writes in his 2014 book, *Citizen Canine: Our Evolving Relationship with Cats and Dogs*, that when beloved family pets died in the 19th century, owners challenged existing beliefs that heaven was meant only for people. "Once an ethereal plane where the departed communed with the almighty, heaven had become a tangible paradise, one populated with familiar scenes of garden and home, and family and friends waiting at the welcome. But where were the pets?" Grimm writes. "Orthodox Christianity, for one, was firm on the issue: only man had an eternal soul. That didn't sit well with a culture increasingly enamored of its cats and dogs."

BETTMANN/GETTY (2)

Growing industrialization fostered the growth of a strong middle class in the West. The mores of the middle-class family included raising children to be exemplary human beings. By bringing a pet into the home, parents hoped to foster wholesome values and caring behavior. A child that was kind and loving to a dog, instead of cruel, was on the right track.

Pets were increasingly entering human hearts, but they were still kept out of our homes. Concerns about fleas and ticks led middle-class homeowners to chain dogs up outside or put them in doghouses. But thanks to grooming products that dealt with these pests, in the 1880s dogs began to move indoors. This spurred a wave of consumer spending. Need to keep Fido from soiling the carpet? There's a book that will tell you how to do that. Want to strengthen his teeth and keep him entertained? Buy a toy. The seeds of today's multibillion-dollar pet industry were sown.

AS OUR DOGS ENTERED THE 20TH century, so did their diets. Feed products for farm animals existed, but for "members of the family," feed was labeled "food." During the Great Depression and the sharp decline of consumer spending, the pet industry wasn't just resilient, it thrived. Dog food sales doubled during the Depression, partly because the 10 cents a can sticker price was more affordable than feeding a dog human food, and also because some impoverished people resorted to an inexpensive product labeled "fit for human consumption."

**With dogs and children spending their days side by side, as seen opposite, keeping pets healthy was crucial. Above: After a rabies outbreak in 1954, Chicago pet owners lined up outside the Illinois Animal Welfare League so that the dogs could receive state-ordered vaccinations.**

Humans also sought out better medical care for their dogs. Before the 20th century, veterinarians were called in only for livestock such as cows or horses—animals that made money. Now pet owners were willing to pay to keep their dear ones safe and healthy.

In the decades of prosperity following World War II, Americans moved from crowded cities to the cleaner and greener suburbs. And as the nuclear family moved into a house with a yard and a white picket fence, dogs began to fill our homes.

Today, 48 percent of households in the United States own at least one dog. Between 2010 and 2016, the percentage of pet owners rose 3 percent, and consumer spending in the pet industry was up more than 25 percent in that same period. Industry specialists like psychology professor Harold Herzog attribute that growth to the boom of luxury pet products, such as gluten-free snacks, doggie day care, and pet fitness trackers.

Why is the pet industry so resilient? It comes down to the special bond between humans and their best friends. "People cut back on vacations, they cut back on the number of times they go out to eat, they cut back on a lot of other things," says Bob Vetere of the American Pet Product Association, "but they're not going to get rid of their pet." The wolf used to inspire fear in our ancestors. Today, we can't imagine life without our canine companions. ■

ELLIOTT ERWITT/MAGNUM

**From the doghouse to our house, Fido has made his way indoors. Although some pet owners believed that keeping their dog outside meant that it would get more exercise, experts dispute that. Dogs, like their wild ancestors, are pack animals and are unhappy in isolation. The Fairbanks family in 1964 knew that life is better together inside.**

# Puppy Love in Middle Age

## A latecomer to dogs discovers the joy

BY CHARLES KRAUTHAMMER

The way I see it, dogs had this big meeting, oh, maybe 20,000 years ago. A huge meeting—an international convention with delegates from everywhere. And that's when they decided that humans were the up-and-coming species and dogs were going to throw their lot in with them. The decision was obviously not unanimous. The wolves and dingoes walked out in protest.

Cats had an even more negative reaction. When they heard the news, they called their own meeting—in Paris, of course—to denounce canine subservience to the human hyperpower. (Their manifesto—*La Condition Feline*—can still be found in provincial bookstores.)

Cats, it must be said, have not done badly. Using guile and seduction, they managed to get humans to feed them, thus preserving their superciliousness without going hungry. A neat trick. Dogs, being guileless, signed and delivered. It was the beginning of a beautiful friendship.

I must admit that I've been slow to warm to dogs. I grew up in a non-pet-friendly home. Dogs do not figure prominently in Jewish-immigrant households. My father was not very high on pets. He wasn't hostile. He just saw them as superfluous, an encumbrance.

MY PARENTS DID ALLOW A HINT OF zoological indulgence. I had a pet turtle. My brother had a parakeet. Both came to unfortunate ends. My turtle fell behind a radiator and was not discovered until too late. And the parakeet, God bless him, flew out a window once, never to be seen again. After such displays of stewardship, we dared not ask for a dog.

My introduction to the wonder of dogs came from my wife, Robyn. She's Australian. And Australia, as lovingly recounted in Bill Bryson's *In a Sunburned Country,* has the craziest, wildest, deadliest, meanest animals on the planet. In a place where every spider and squid can take you down faster than a sucker punched boxer, you cherish niceness in the animal kingdom. And they don't come nicer than dogs.

**"When the Man waked up he said, 'What is Wild Dog doing here?' And the Woman said, 'His name is not Wild Dog anymore, but the First Friend, because he will be our friend for always and always and always.'" —Rudyard Kipling, *The Jungle Book***

ZAK KENDAL/CULTURA/AURORA

FLORIAN GAERTNER/PHOTOTHEK/GETTY

Robyn started us off slowly. She got us a border collie, Hugo, when our son was about six. She knew that would appeal to me because the border collie is the smartest species on the planet. Hugo could 1) play outfield in our backyard baseball games, 2) do flawless front-door sentry duty, and 3) play psychic weatherman, announcing with a wail every coming thunderstorm.

WHEN OUR SON, DANIEL, TURNED 10, he wanted a dog of his own. I was against it, using arguments borrowed from seminars on nuclear nonproliferation. It was hopeless. One giant "Please, Dad," and I caved completely. Robyn went out to Winchester, Virginia, found a litter of black Labs and brought home Chester.

But it was Chester, who dispensed affection as unreflectively as he breathed, who got me thinking about this long-ago pact between humans and dogs. Cat lovers and the pet averse will just roll their eyes at such dogophilia. I can't help it. Chester was always at your foot or your hand, waiting to be petted and stroked, played with and talked to. His beautiful blocky head, his wonderful overgrown puppy's body, his baritone bark filled every corner of house and heart.

At the tender age of eight, he died quite suddenly. The long, slobbering, slothful decline we had been looking forward to was not to be. When told the news, a young friend who was a regular victim of Chester's lunging love-bombs said mournfully, "He was the sweetest creature I ever saw. He's the only dog I ever saw kiss a cat."

Some will protest that in a world with so much human suffering, it is something between eccentric and obscene to mourn a dog. I think not. After all, it is perfectly normal, indeed, deeply human to be moved when nature presents us with a vision of great beauty. Should we not be moved when it produces a vision—a creature—of the purest sweetness? ■

**"Dogs are our link to paradise. They don't know evil or jealousy or discontent. To sit with a dog on a hillside on a glorious afternoon is to be back in Eden, where doing nothing was not boring — it was peace." —author Milan Kundera**

H. ARMSTRONG ROBERTS/CLASSICSTOCK/AURORA

# A Healing Touch

**Sometimes they're trained to help with specific tasks. Others help by just being present. All of these dogs provide special care to those in need**

This comfort dog, named Peter Parker (after Spider-Man's alter ego), works with speech therapy students at New York City's Park Place Community Middle School.

# At Our Service

## From sniffing out diseases to leading the blind, these dogs are trained to aid those in need

BY LISA RUSSELL

Karen Shirk remembers well the evening that was nearly her last. Already suffering from the rare neuromuscular disease myasthenia gravis and confined to a wheelchair, she was at her Ohio home following open-heart surgery, with her trusted service dog, Ben, a black Lab, by her side. "I was on a morphine pump and—though I didn't realize it—a deadly combination of drugs," Shirk told the *New York Times*. "I slipped into unconsciousness." Then the phone rang. Sensing something was wrong, Ben picked up the receiver, dropped it on the bed, and started barking. The caller was Shirk's father, who got Ben's message loud and clear and summoned a rescue team to his daughter's house. The rescuers later told Karen that without Ben's quick thinking she wouldn't have lived through the night.

A typical day for Ben and the estimated 200,000 service dogs in America is much more mundane but no less heroic. It is spent helping their owners navigate life's daily ups and downs, which may be made steeper by ailments ranging from severe allergies to missing limbs to crippling anxiety.

Beyond the familiar vest-wearing guide dogs for the blind, service dogs (who often but not always wear vests) come in an array of specialties: Allergy dogs are trained to be ultrasensitive to the presence of life-threatening allergens; diabetic-alert dogs can detect by smell when their human's blood sugar level gets dangerously low. A brace/mobility support dog, who must be big enough to carry the weight of its owner, prevents slips and falls for those with balance issues, and medical-alert dogs jump into action if the person at the other end of the leash suffers a seizure. And while many service dogs assist people with missing limbs or visible mobility issues, "some disabilities, like many neurological disorders or the cardiac condition POTS [postural orthostatic tachycardia syndrome, which can cause fainting], are invisible and may not be apparent to others," according to the website for Anything Is Pawsable, an organization that helps service dog owners, trainers, and breeders.

EITAN ABRAMOVICH/AFP/GETTY

**With the help of his service dog, autistic seven-year-old Juan Pablo Torena rode the subway for the first time in Buenos Aires, Argentina, in April 2016.**

BILL CLARK/ROLL CALL/GETTY

Service dogs are different from therapy dogs (often brought to sites to help people deal with grief and tension) and emotional support animals (ESAs, who typically aid just one person). According to the Americans with Disabilities Act (ADA), service dogs are those that have been specially trained—at a cost of up to $35,000 and with some 500 hours of training—to perform helping tasks specific to the owner's disability. Therapy dogs and ESAs may or may not be formally trained; they aid people simply by their presence. Service animals are "working animals," not pets, according to Justice Department ADA requirements, giving them the right to be in pretty much any public space. ADA regulations state that "dogs whose sole function is to provide comfort or emotional support do not qualify as service animals under the ADA."

So while true service dogs are legal in restaurants and bowling alleys, therapy and ESA dogs technically aren't. Unfortunately, that technicality is often ignored by pet owners who want to take their dogs with them everywhere. "Their animals aren't trained and end up misbehaving in these public places, which give real service dogs a bad name," says state representative Kimberly Ferguson of Massachusetts, one of 19 states to enact laws cracking down on fake service pets.

WHEN IT COMES TO A GOOD SERVICE dog, size matters. Too small and they won't be of much physical help to their human. Too big and they can't fit under a restaurant table inconspicuously. "Over time, we found that roughly 70 percent of Labradors, golden retrievers, and German shepherds graduated from our program, while only about 2 percent of other breeds make the cut," says one trainer. When it comes to temperament, the best service dogs are friendly, people-oriented, calm, and not too active. They are confident, neither dominant nor submissive, and trainable.

More and more, the child-canine connection is proving to be strong medicine, especially in dealing with autism. A child or teen in the midst of a meltdown will often respond best to their canine

CONTINUED ON PAGE 47

**Seeing Eye dog Gillian helps Army veteran Joseph Bogart, above. Bogart was blinded by a bomb explosion in Iraq in 2006. Opposite: Andrew Cosell of Long Island, New York, who suffers from cerebral palsy, relies on his K-9 companion retriever, Charger.**

TOM NEBBIA

3

JAMES SALZANO

JUSTIN SULLIVAN/GETTY

ARTERRA/UIG/GETTY

**Michael Hingson and Seeing Eye dog Roselle, left, outside their Westfield, New Jersey, home. Both are survivors of the 9/11 terrorist attack on the World Trade Center. Top: Paralyzed Army vet Andrew Pike watched Yazmin practice turning on a light at the Canine Companions for Independence training center in Santa Rosa, California. Above: A mobility assistance dog helped out at a supermarket in Belgium.**

Z

During a 2016 Boston Red Sox game against the Baltimore Orioles, war veteran K.J. and his service dog, Hope, shared a moment at Fenway Park.

MELANIE STETSON FREEMAN/THE CHRISTIAN SCIENCE MONITOR/GETTY

CONTINUED FROM PAGE 42

companion gently getting them down on the floor and calmly and firmly lying on top of them, literally covering them with comfort. But those on the autism spectrum are hardly alone. "We place dogs with kids in wheelchairs, kids on ventilators, kids with autism, kids with dwarfism, kids with seizure disorder and cognitive impairments," says Karen Shirk, who, inspired by her experience with Ben, founded 4 Paws for Ability, a nonprofit service dog training school in Xenia, Ohio.

Shirk says that Ben's presence helped her open up social connections after years of loneliness, so she knows from experience that "kids will ignore your disability if you've got a cool dog." Taxi, a golden retriever service dog, became such a beloved part of Rachel Benke's private and public life in San Antonio, where Taxi was on alert for the eighth grader's epileptic seizures, that he earned his own photo in Benke's Hector Garcia Middle School yearbook. "It's been fun," Benke's mom, Teresa, told the *Today* show. "And it's been even more fun watching [Rachel] get excited about it."

And then there are the 53,000 American soldiers who've been physically wounded in Afghanistan and Iraq, and the some 300,000 suffering the invisible agonies of post-traumatic stress disorder. More than any other single war injury, PTSD has proved that adults in emotional crisis are just as likely as kids to benefit from the trust, loyalty, and canine competence of a service dog. Veterans have sought help from groups like Pets for Vets and K9s for Warriors, two nonprofits that pair PTSD sufferers with rescue dogs trained to become service dogs. So far, K9s for Warriors has graduated more than 300 "teams" of "battle buddies." A vet named Karen graduated from the group's three-week training camp in March 2017 with her service dog, George. "[He] was a rescue, and I am so thankful they saved his life," she said of K9s. "In turn, he has saved my life." ■

# Being There

## Therapy dogs can heal simply by their presence

BY AMY LENNARD GOEHNER

Once it was illegal for dogs to enter a hospital. Today they are a welcome part of the healing process. Good Dog Foundation founder Rachel McPherson recalls when she put her own therapy dog, a tricolor papillon named Fidel, to work at one New York City hospital not long ago. A patient was recuperating from a stroke and had no movement on his left side. McPherson taught little Fidel to jump on the patient's bed and drop her ball next to the man's left hand. Little by little the patient was able to gain movement in his left hand to the point where he was able to toss the ball for Fidel to retrieve. "He was motivated by the joy Fidel brought him," says McPherson. "When the physical therapists showed up, he'd say, 'I need Fidel.'" In time, the patient regained movement on his whole left side.

It's no wonder hospitals have seen an increase in requests for therapy dogs within the last decade. Providing comfort is at the heart of what therapy dogs do in the myriad places where they are called to action. People who work with these dogs describe the "unconditional love" and psychological healing they bring to people who are suffering or faced with stressful situations—just by virtue of their presence.

Among the people and places the dogs and their owners or handlers visit are patients in hospitals and hospices, the elderly, students with and without disabilities, and families at morgues, funerals, and disaster sites. The dogs provide much-needed comfort to victims, their families, and responders.

The sense of comfort that kids feel in classrooms where therapy dogs visit has been proven to have a positive impact on learning. A 2017 study by Tufts University's Institute for Human-Animal Interaction concluded that second graders who read aloud to dogs—thus eliminating the stress or fear of judgment by peers—showed improved attitudes about reading. Just reading to a dog becomes a motivating factor in itself.

Nine-year-old Bolo Guialdo is one of several children with autism whose reading skills have improved since

ARTERRA/UIG/GETTY

Therapy dogs can be any breed or size, but they need to be well behaved, housebroken, and friendly around people.

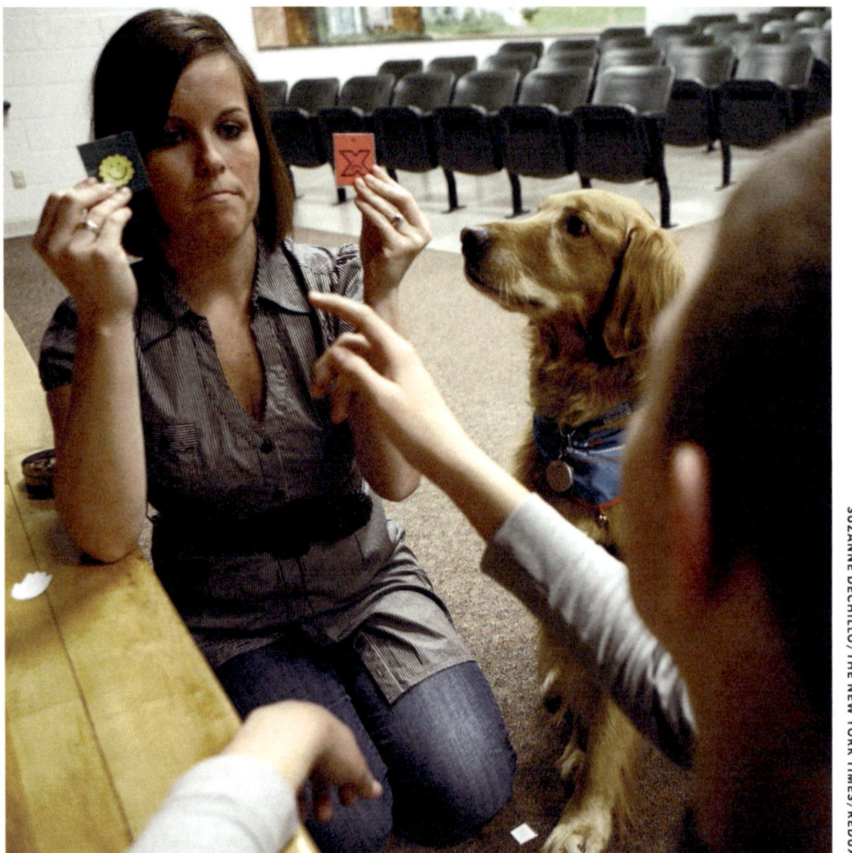

SUZANNE DECHILLO/THE NEW YORK TIMES/REDUX

a therapy dog, in his case a French bulldog named Lucky, came to his class. Bolo says Lucky makes him feel "relaxed," and Bolo's dad, Ron, says that just getting to be with Lucky has motivated Bolo to do his tasks in the morning in order to get to school. "It's more than just reading," adds Ron. "The dog has helped Bolo get his life in order."

Children who have been victims of abuse and must tell their stories in court find the process easier with a therapy dog by their side. Last year, responding to a growing trend, Florida enacted a law that allows therapy dogs to be present in all state courts. For children, having a soft, calming dog they can pat as they go through the trauma of telling their stories—often while facing their accused abusers—can be tremendously beneficial.

NOT EVERY DOG HAS WHAT IT TAKES to become a therapy dog. The single most important factor is temperament. A dog must be friendly, gentle, and obedient, and be unflappable in noisy, chaotic, and unpredictable environments. It must be comfortable with other animals and enjoy being petted and hugged by unfamiliar people. One program renowned for its rigorous hands-on training is the Good Dog Foundation, which services four East Coast states. Dogs are first evaluated for temperament and other basic traits, and if they pass (about half do) they qualify for a six-week therapy-skills program, which includes several sessions in simulated environments, such as a hospital setting with I.V. poles and people in wheelchairs.

Dogs as small as nine-pound Fidel or as large as a 50-plus-pound German shepherd—both purebreds and mixed breeds—can become therapy dogs. Lily, for example, is a pit bull who was found wandering—most likely tossed from a car—on a busy New York City highway during rush hour. She was rescued by police and soon adopted. Her new owner, Katie Vogelsang, says that given Lily's trauma, she and her husband were prepared to just let Lily hang out—that is until Lily gave them a look that said, as Vogelsang put it, "I'm good, guys, what's next?" So Lily became a therapy dog and now visits shelters and schools.

LUKA DAKSKOBLER/XINHUA/EYEVINE/REDUX

**Opposite: Therapy dog Dutchess and occupational therapist assistant Courtney Peggs worked with a client at the Anderson Center for Autism in Staatsburg, New York. Above: Shanti, a reading education assistance dog, calmed Mihael as he read, in Krani, Slovenia. The Reading Education Assistance Dog program operates throughout Slovenia.**

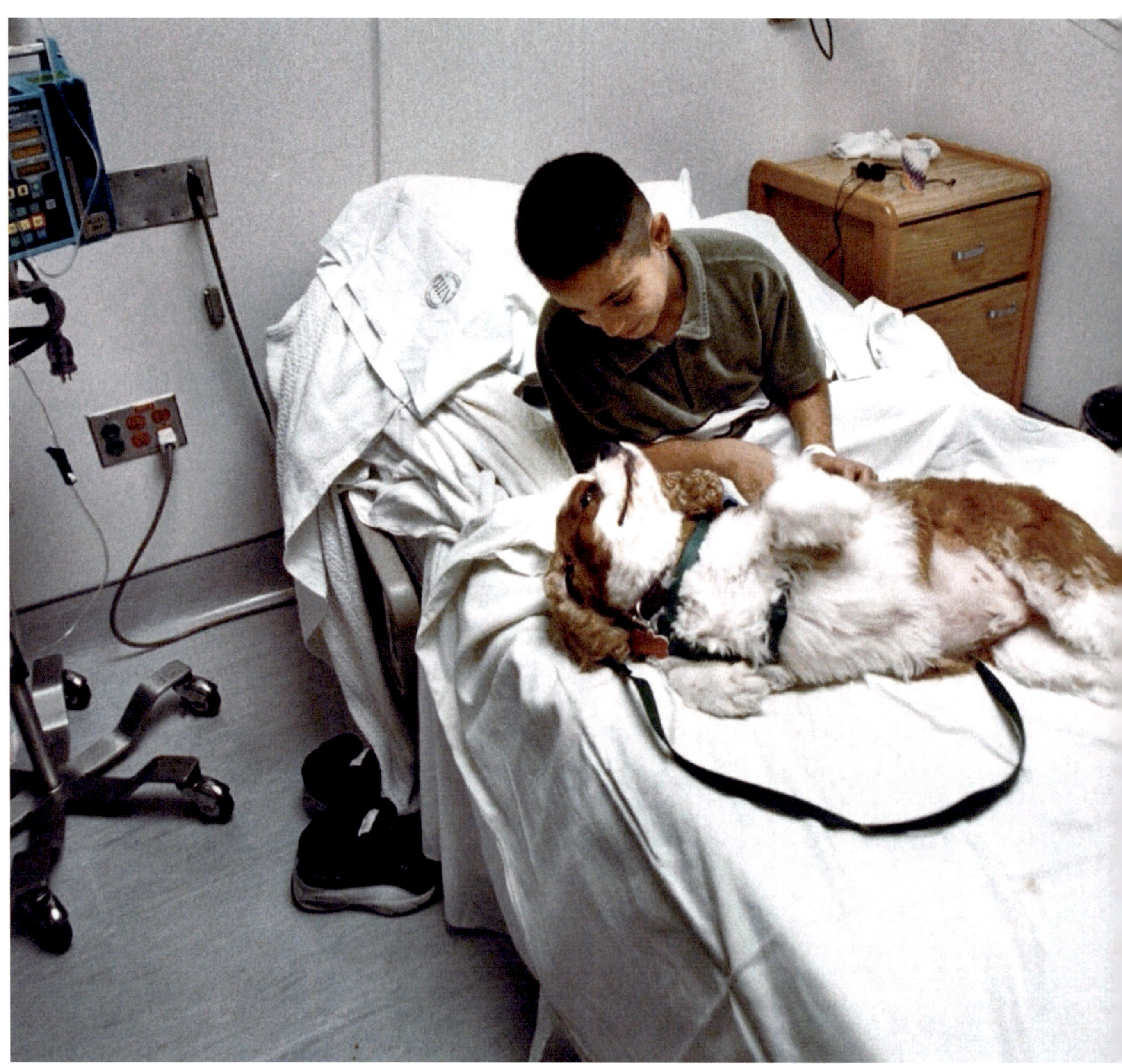

In one elementary school classroom, Vogelsang talked to kids about Lily's mistreatment and the meaning of the word *abandoned,* leading one girl to tell the class that her family lived in a shelter. "She shared that with us, she felt comfortable," said Vogelsang.

THE COMFORT THAT DOGS BRING IS more than anecdotal. In a first-of-its-kind study, Dr. Stewart Fleishman of Mount Sinai Beth Israel Hospital in New York City selected a number of patients with head and neck cancer who faced six weeks of taxing treatment, including chemotherapy and radiation. He had therapy dogs visit them during their treatment sessions. The result? Even as patients suffered physically from the side effects of their treatment, their emotional well-being, as measured in the study, was high. Patients would arrive at sessions upbeat and even playful. One patient told Dr. Fleishman, "If not for the dog, I would have stopped coming three weeks ago." And in other studies, the National Institutes of Health concluded that just interacting with a dog can lower blood pressure and decrease stress.

Perhaps no one knows more about stress than first responders, such as police and firefighters. Retired New York City Police Department lieutenant Grace Telesco was on her way to teach a college class in crisis intervention when the first plane hit the World Trade Center north tower on 9/11. She was subsequently deployed to run the Family Assistance Center, where the families of those who died received crisis-intervention services. One of Telesco's responsibilities was to bring family members several days later to Ground Zero to visit the spot where their loved ones had perished. She insisted therapy dogs accompany the group. "I watched families who would

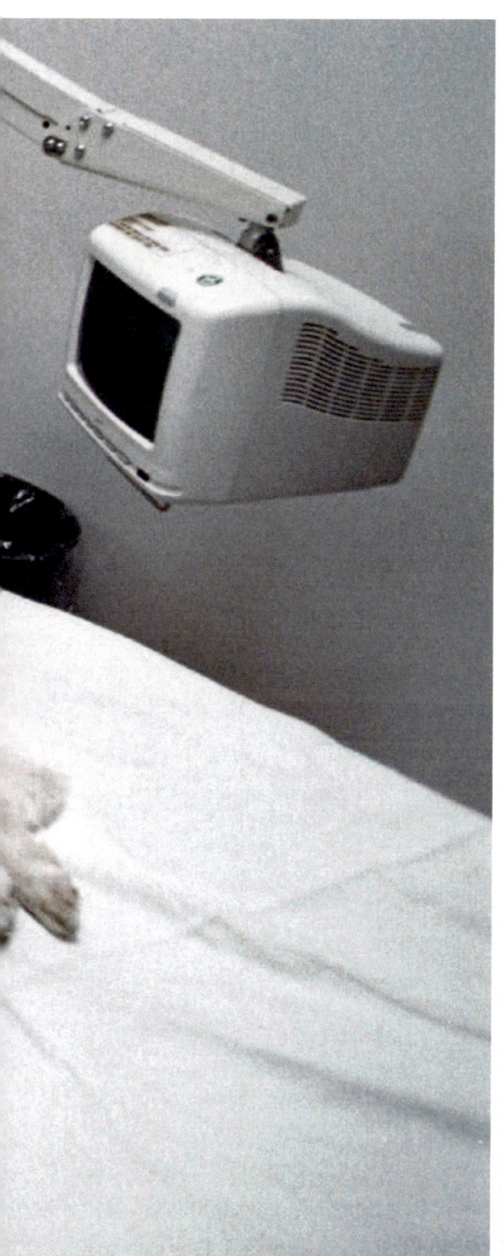

TODD HEISLER/THE NEW YORK TIMES/REDUX

CAROL GUZY/THE WASHINGTON POST/GETTY

not respond to a mental health worker or a cop open up and just fall apart on the dogs," Telesco says.

When therapy dogs arrive at a disaster site, the comfort and bonhomie they spread is equally felt—and needed—by victims, their families, and rescuers. "I personally needed to hug these dogs. I know the magic of dogs, I know the medicine. If you want to know how to be a crisis intervention specialist, just look at how the therapy dogs handled it," recalls Telesco. "What did they do? They were just *present*—this unconditional, loving, supportive presence for the families." ■

**Therapy dog Scooter comforted 10-year-old Timm Jackson at the National Institutes of Health, above left. Scooter was part of a group visiting the hospital from Delta Society National Capital Therapy Dogs. Above, right: Former naval officer Tori Stitt received comfort from Devon, who offers relief from some of the effects of post-traumatic stress disorder.**

# We've Got Their Backs

## In times of need, people mobilize to help dogs that cannot help themselves

BY COURTNEY MIFSUD

In the remote central mountains of New Guinea, one of the most inhospitable regions on earth, 15 highland wild dogs were spotted by members of a 2016 expedition that was searching for the dogs. These dogs, isolated from human contact, are considered the rarest in the world, almost impossible to find in the wild. The short-haired dogs have pointed ears, weigh about 25 pounds, and are known for their unique howl, which they perform in unison.

Only about 300 of these dogs remain in the world, in zoos and in private homes. Until the recent expedition, they were thought to be extinct in the wild. Local mining companies have partnered with the expedition researchers and taken steps to preserve the ecosystem around mining facilities, creating a sanctuary where these singing dogs can survive. These conservation efforts, along with ongoing scientific studies and public education, have been critical to maintaining the genetic diversity and overall health of the rare breed. Ensuring that endangered species are protected is just one of the many ways that people work to protect dogs.

Humans take the role of protector seriously, and that extends beyond the reaches of New Guinea. Approximately 3.3 million dogs enter U.S. animal shelters every year. The Humane Society and the American Society for the Prevention of Cruelty to Animals (ASPCA) work to keep dogs off the streets and in loving homes. The efforts are paying off: Since 2011, increasing numbers of animals have been adopted and more lost animals have been returned to their owners.

Many agencies, such as the ASPCA, work with law enforcement on rescue missions to save endangered pets. When the police get wind of a potential cruelty case, they'll contact animal protection agencies to coordinate a raid and share expertise. While it's up to law enforcement to obtain the necessary warrants and execute the search, animal welfare groups participate to make sure that any recovered animal is given immediate medical attention. If the agency becomes the guardian of the rescued animal, it will see to it that the

After Hurricane Harvey pounded southeast Texas in 2017, Megan Lowry, from the Wounded Veterans of Oklahoma, rescued a puppy from a flooded home in Orange, Texas.

SCOTT OLSON/GETTY

dog is placed with a suitable household.

In January 2016, responders from the ASPCA mobilized in Raeford, North Carolina. The Hoke County Sheriff's Office and the North Carolina Department of Agriculture had reached out to the rescue group for help. Law enforcement had been investigating an unlicensed adoption facility called the Haven after receiving numerous complaints that animals adopted from the 122-acre site were sick. The facility had limited protection from the elements, and animals' medical issues went untreated. After law enforcement arrested the owners, the ASPCA removed more than 700 dogs, cats, horses, and pigs. "This is one of the largest animal seizures the ASPCA has ever conducted in our 150 years as an organization," Tim Rickey, ASPCA senior vice president of field investigations and response, said at the time. "We have a team of more than 130 responders on the ground to remove and care for these hundreds of neglected animals who have clearly not been receiving adequate care. Our goal is to help them become healthy and ultimately find them homes." The organization housed the animals at a local temporary shelter, where they received medical evaluations and care.

EVEN WHEN A DOG HAS A PROTECTIVE forever family, the unexpected can still happen, and heroes step in to meet needs. The number of humans living in disaster-prone areas is growing, along with the number of natural disasters.

**When a massive earthquake rattled China in 2008, a Sichuan province animal-rescue center sheltered more than 100 stray dogs and cats from affected areas. The center fitted disabled dogs with cartlike "wheelchairs," above. Opposite: Firefighter Chris Klein gave oxygen to Fancy, a dog rescued from a 2007 Brooklyn apartment fire. Along with Fancy, the three human residents of the eighth floor apartment were also rescued.**

CHINA PHOTOS/GETTY

DEBBIE EGAN-CHIN/NY DAILY NEWS ARCHIVE/GETTY

In 2006, in the wake of Hurricane Katrina, Congress passed the Pets Evacuation and Transportation Standards (PETS) Act. This legislation requires that states requesting FEMA assistance have adequate plans in place to evacuate service animals and pets. The PETS Act also allows FEMA to provide assistance, shelter, and relief where possible. "There's been a shift in the way we treat animals, particularly in the past couple of decades," says Dian Fowles, who investigated human-animal relations in the wake of natural disasters in 2014. "As the recognition of the human-animal connection grows stronger, it's important to understand how these relationships can be tested during times of disaster."

Although organizations are in place to reunite pets and their owners after a hurricane, tornado, or fire, the Centers for Disease Control advises pet owners to take early precautions like microchipping pets and having an individual carrier for each animal.

IN THE PAST DECADE, MEDICAL advancements for dogs have stayed on track with health breakthroughs for humans. Pet supplements such as multivitamins and probiotics allow dogs to reap benefits previously available only to people. Advancements in DNA testing allow dog owners to identify genes that could lead to illness in certain breeds. CT scanners and MRI machines are now in animal hospitals.

Even the doctors have changed. In previous decades, a veterinarian was a generalist whose only option for a seriously ill animal might have been euthanasia. Today, the modern vet may be a specialist in one of 40 fields, such as oncology or cardiology, who can offer advanced treatments. The progress in veterinary medicine has led to healthier and longer lives for dogs. ■

# Photo Shoot

## Camera-ready pooches come in all shapes and sizes

**Real Lookers**
Basset hounds, opposite, are known for their powerful sense of smell, second only to that of bloodhounds. Mutts, like this husky-mix puppy, make up 53 percent of the U.S. dog population.

ADRIANO BACCHELLA/NPL/MINDEN

MARK RAYCROFT/MINDEN

MINDY SCHAUER/THE ORANGE COUNTY REGISTER/ZUMA

**Best in Show**

**Opposite: Two popular breeds, a cocker spaniel, top, and a boxer. Above: Jimmy Stewart and Rita Hayworth are two poodles that assist California child psychologist Amy Stark. These therapy dogs stand nearly four feet tall. Their calming and comforting presence helps kids and teens deal with the stresses of divorce and other family upheavals.**

COLIN MONTEATH/HEDGEHOG HOUSE/MINDEN

## Rise and Shine

**Above: This Siberian husky rested during an east-west traverse of the Greenland ice cap. Three husky teams from Norway pulling wooden sledges accompanied five skiers on the 600-kilometer journey. Opposite, top: Pugs are one of the oldest dog breeds and can be traced back 2,000 years. Bottom: Labradoodle Belle is a mix of a standard poodle and a Labrador retriever.**

MARK RAYCROFT/MINDEN

JEFF MINTON

British Army corporals Marianne Hay and Dave Heyhoe with their dogs Leanna and Treo in a 2008 Allied mission to capture Taliban leaders in Afghanistan.

MARCO DI LAURO/GETTY

# To Protect and to Serve

**Whether teaming with soldiers overseas or sniffing out crime within our own borders, these dogs work to keep us safe**

# Four-Legged Heroes

## These dogs put their lives on the line every day to protect soldiers in the armed forces

BY DAN BOVA

In the corner of a room in an Afghanistan compound, behind a pile of sandbags, an insurgent fighter sat with his finger on the trigger of a belt-fed Russian machine gun. A unit of American soldiers was searching for him, and he planned to open fire as soon as they stepped through the door.

That plan never had a chance, however, thanks to the first brave American to step in the room: a working dog named Arko.

The insurgent was no match for Arko's speed and ferocity. Arko instantly launched himself at the man behind the machine gun, biting him in the bicep and taking him down before he could fire a single shot at the soldiers pouring into the room.

In the heat of their struggle, the insurgent was able to grab the AK-47 he had on his back and shoot Arko in the chest. Still, Arko held his grip until the men in his unit were able to dispatch the bad guy.

There is no doubt that Arko saved the lives of the American soldiers in that room. And thanks to fast medical attention, the hero dog lived to bark another day.

ARKO IS A SPECIAL DOG IN A RICH tradition of canines giving invaluable aid to their human counterparts during times of conflict. Documentation from 600 BCE describes how Alyattes, king of Lydia, unleashed dogs on an invading Cimmerian army. "These fell upon the invaders and tore many of them to pieces and put others to flight," reads the text.

Throughout history, warrior dogs have distinguished themselves with displays of bravery, intelligence, and loyalty. Probably the most famous four-legged war hero is Stubby, an American pit bull terrier who served alongside the men of the 102nd Infantry Regiment in the front line trenches of France during World War I. During Stubby's time in the field, he suffered injury from a gas attack. After medical treatment, he returned to the trenches, with a high sensitivity to the smell of gas. That sensitivity alerted him to a gas attack one early morning when the troops were asleep. Stubby barked and

BRYCE HARPER/THE NEW YORK TIMES/REDUX

Airman Dereck Stevens and his working dog, seen here before a drill at San Antonio's Lackland Air Force Base, share a bond that extends beyond battle.

GRANGER

nipped at his compatriots to wake them up, saving many from the horrifying effects of the chemical weapon. Stubby was also noted for his ability to find injured soldiers and was credited with attacking and subduing a German spy. For his actions, Stubby was promoted to Sergeant Stubby, the first dog to be given rank in the U.S. armed forces, according to the Smithsonian National Museum of American History.

World War II saw a big leap in the use of dogs in the military—initially as sentry dogs to guard against attacks by enemy saboteurs on U.S. installations overseas and at home. Citizen dog breeders and experts formed Dogs for Defense Inc., a program funded by the American Kennel Club and individual donors to procure and train the animals for duty. Over the course of the war, Dogs for Defense helped find and train approximately 20,000 dogs for the effort.

As the war changed course, so did the role of the dogs. The threat of enemies arriving on U.S. soil via submarine subsided, and while many of the overseas sentry dogs were returned home, some were trained to take on roles in tactical operations, working as scouts and messengers, pulling sleds, and aiding in mine detection. The ongoing experiment produced promising results—and many incredible fighters. One dog, a messenger named Sandy, ran through tall grass, swam a river, dodged mortar and tank fire, and leaped over barbed wire to deliver a message to an artillery unit, saving the lives and advancing a line of U.S. troops pinned down by Japanese fortifications.

Training programs for dogs and their handlers continued to grow, but it wasn't until the Vietnam War that the training became formalized. "Vietnam is really when we established the dog school at the Lackland Air Force Base in San Antonio," explains Doug Miller, the Working Dog Program manager for the Department of Defense. "That's when the Air Force became the executive agent for the dogs, training and deploying them to all branches, including Special Operations Forces and the Pentagon Force Protection Agency."

In Vietnam, military working dogs were trained and used for a variety of tasks: providing security on bases,

NATIONAL GEOGRAPHIC STOCK: VINTAGE COLLECTION/GRANGER

World War I hero Stubby, opposite, took part in a parade in Washington, D.C., in 1921. After retiring from service, Stubby and his master, Corporal Robert Conroy, went on to Georgetown University Law Center, where the dog became the team mascot of the Georgetown Hoyas. Many other dogs served in the war, including messenger dogs, above, hurdling trenches to relay information across the battlefield.

**During the Vietnam War, Christian Dietz (opposite) followed Wolf, his scout dog, in a search for enemy troops. Above: American GIs treated a wounded combat dog during World War II.**

AP/REX/SHUTTERSTOCK

detecting ambushes on patrol, and hunting down retreating enemy soldiers in the thick of battle. Richard Cunningham, a dog handler who served in Vietnam from 1967 to 1968, called these dogs "the gold standard" for troop safety in an essay he wrote for the *New York Times*. "Search-and-destroy missions used a handler and his scout dog to walk point, out in the jungle, able to raise an alarm about an ambush long before most of the unit was in danger." These elite working dogs, Cunningham wrote, had a remarkable knack for spotting monofilament lines used to trip enemy booby traps and mines that maimed and killed U.S. troops with horrific effectiveness. "I've heard it said that without our military dogs, there would be 10,000 additional names on the Vietnam Veterans Memorial wall," Cunningham wrote. "I, for one, think that's an understatement."

There are 1,800 working dogs currently serving alongside U.S. military men and women throughout the world, all trained by the 341st Training Squadron at Lackland Air Force Base. Their role, and the level at which they perform, has increased tremendously.

"In the past, the more typical role was that of a sentry dog," says Miller. "They would be guarding a fence line or an area—they were pretty much attack dogs that would not come off unless you pulled them off. The patrol dogs now, you can call them off even before they make a bite, or you can call off even after they make a bite, as long as the person stops struggling."

These dogs have a well-earned reputation as animals you don't want to mess with, and oftentimes no bites are required to bring down the bad guys, according to Master Sergeant Kevin Bartoo, Air Force Military Working Dog Program manager. "Sometimes the simple presence of these dogs is a psychological deterrent," he says. "When a K-9 unit shows up and somebody is thinking about doing something wrong, that tends to make them stop and think, 'Hey, do I really want to get bit right now?' And that can be enough to stop people from doing what they were going to do, or were in the middle of doing."

Miller says that nearly all of the dogs trained at Lackland come from breeders in Eastern Europe. They primarily use three breeds: Dutch shepherd, German shepherd, and Belgian Malinois. "Over the last 10 to 15 years, we've turned to the Belgian more as our dog of choice," Miller says. "They don't seem to have the hip problems and lumbar problems some shepherds have had. And while they're not quite as heavy a lot of times as the shepherds, they are just as fast, lean, and mean. We call them 'maligators' as puppies

Above: At Lackland Air Force Base, Staff Sergeant Shane Larsen and his working dog went through a warehouse drill in 2011. Opposite: Sniffer dog Ben and his handler, Rusty Smith, checked for explosives during a 2002 training demonstration at Lackland.

BRYCE HARPER/THE NEW YORK TIMES/REDUX

BRYCE HARPER/GETTY

because they are just so driven."

The dogs go through careful assessment by the trainers of the 341st. They are checked to see if they exhibit fear of strangers or aversion to noises or hesitancy when confronted with environmental obstacles. In one test, assessors throw a ball out into tall weeds and see if the dog will give up or continue to search until they find it. "They want to see what kind of drive the dog has," says Miller.

Depending on the mission and tasks, training can take up to a year, and typically dogs get to the field around the age of two. The DOD invests approximately $40,000 in each dog it develops to work. That is a small price when you consider the American lives they've saved.

Most working dogs serve an average of six years, says Master Sergeant Bartoo. "You sometimes have a dog that goes until they are 13 or 14 years old, but those are rarities. Typically around eight or nine is when we really start to look at the quality of life for the dog."

THE DOGS ARE PARTICULARLY GOOD at finding bad guys and bombs thanks to their brawn and their noses, says former Navy SEAL Mike Ritland, founder of both Trikos International, a company that trains working dogs, and the Warrior Dog Foundation, which provides care for dogs after they retire. Ritland describes the dogs' remarkable capabilities. "These dogs can detect human odor quite a ways away. So they're very good at anti-ambush operations and finding insurgents who are hiding under false floors or fake furniture or under piles of laundry. They're better than us with detection," he says, "and since they're smaller, lighter, and faster than us, they are incredibly impactful when it comes time to take down and neutralize these threats. Insurgents are not expecting a dog to come flying through a window or a door at 28 miles per hour and it catches them off guard."

Dogs are key assets for soldiers dealing with "squirters"—enemies who bolt from the back of a house during a gunfight. "The dog bumps out during a raid and takes a flank and if [an enemy combatant] bails out the back and takes off, they'll send the dog from there and be able to catch him," explains Ritland. "And the nice thing about the dogs that gets overlooked or understated is that they are a nonlethal force protection measure."

The impact of dogs sniffing out IEDs (improvised explosive devices) is especially notable. "They'll find buried artillery shells or big barrels filled with hundreds of pounds of cooked-down homemade explosives. It's impossible to quantify how many lives they've saved, but it is undoubtedly thousands of lives at this point."

Just as soldiers can be distinguished for standout work, so can dogs. A U.S. Marine working dog named Lucca was recently given special recognition for her efforts. Over the course of three combat tours in Afghanistan and Iraq, Lucca led more than 400 patrols and is credited with at least 40 confirmed discoveries of enemy combatants, explosives, and ammunition—and for having no human casualties on her watch. On what would be her last mission, Lucca sniffed out a 30-pound explosive device that would have brought death and dismemberment to the men in her unit. While searching for more IEDs, a second bomb exploded, badly burning Lucca and leading to the eventual amputation of her front leg. Lucca recovered from her injuries, and in 2016 the trustees of the People's Dispensary for Sick Animals unanimously voted to award Lucca the Dickin Medal, the animal equivalent of the Victoria Cross, the United Kingdom's highest award for valor. She is the first U.S. Marine Corps dog to receive the honor.

SO WHAT COMES NEXT FOR THESE dogs who have served, often at the cost of physical and psychological damage? That's where Mike Ritland's Warrior Dog Foundation steps in. One of a handful of organizations dedicated to providing care for retired working dogs, the Warrior Dog Foundation's mission is three-pronged, Ritland says: First and foremost, its mission is to prevent the dogs from being

DAVID CHESKIN/PA IMAGES/GETTY

**Denzil leads gunner Simon Stupple on a 2003 patrol near Umm Qsar, an Iraqi port. The Iraq war was the first time in three decades that the U.S. had used war dogs.**

SGT. ALFRED V. LOPEZ/USMC/MCT/GETTY

FRANK AUGSTEIN/AP/REX/SHUTTERSTOCK

euthanized and to give them a healthy place to live in dignity. Second is to evaluate them and see if they can be rehabilitated and given a new home. Third, if the dog is young and fit enough, is to find it a new job working with the police, border patrol, or other area of law enforcement.

Often, while the dogs are in rehab, their original handlers will visit. "It's very emotional," says Ritland. "It's really similar to the videos you see of troops coming home and surprising their kids at high school football games and stuff like that. It's a hard thing for outside people to understand—the bond that forms between these people and these dogs. It's forged in these intense combat experiences, life-and-death experiences. For the handlers, these are dogs they know firsthand have saved their lives or gotten injured saving other team members' lives. There just aren't any words to describe these reunions."

Miller from the DOD has seen his share of reunions between dogs and their handlers at Lackland, and one that has stayed with him involves a dog named Bronco. While serving in Afghanistan, Bronco was out on a Special Operations Forces mission with his handler. As they were walking, they came upon an enemy who was wielding an AK-47. The handler unclipped Bronco, who fearlessly attacked the enemy and rendered him helpless. In the midst of their struggle, Bronco was shot in the face by the insurgent. The dog ran off, and his handler thought he was dead. After the enemy was dispatched, the unit followed a blood trail and found Bronco sitting behind a wall. They were able to get the dog medevaced to the human hospital in Kandahar, where he was treated and sent on for more care. Bronco eventually wound up back at Lackland and had more reconstructive surgery. "In the end, Bronco's handler came to visit and adopted him," says Miller. "The bond that forms between handlers and these dogs is like that of a parent and child. The dog is totally dependent on you for care and feeding, but usually your child is not going to defend you from the enemy. And that's what these dogs are ready and willing to do every day of their lives." ■

Marine Lance Corporal Brandon Mann and his detection dog, Ty, patrolled a village in Afghanistan in 2012, opposite. Awarded the Dickin Medal by the People's Dispensary for Sick Animals in 2016 for her bravery, U.S. Marine dog Lucca, above, lost a leg in the course of protecting thousands of troops in Afghanistan and Iraq on more than 400 missions.

# Keeping the Peace

## These K-9s work hard to detect danger, rescue victims, and sniff out crime

BY RICHARD JEROME

In New York City, at the National September 11 Memorial & Museum no exhibit is more powerful than the personal property collection—victims' wallets, phones, watches, jewelry, and other possessions pulled from the ruins of the World Trade Center. Among these ordinary yet deeply moving artifacts are a leash, an animal hair brush, and a Port Authority Police Department badge that reads "K-9 17." These items relate to a yellow Labrador retriever named Sirius—the only police dog killed with some 3,000 people in the worst terrorist attack on U.S. soil. Sirius and his partner, PAPD lieutenant David Lim, were in the basement of the south tower at 8:45 a.m. that cloudless Tuesday morning when they experienced a violent jolt: Hijacked American Airlines flight 11 had crashed into the adjacent north tower. After first securing Sirius in his south tower kennel, Lim hurried off to investigate. "I'll come back to you, I promise," he recalled telling his partner. "That was the last I saw of him."

Dashing to the north tower, Lim scrambled up to the 44th floor and pitched in to shepherd terrified occupants to safety. He was guiding Brooklyn grandmother Josephine Harris down stairwell B when, amid the sickening sounds of the crushing of steel, concrete, and humanity, the 110-story building collapsed. Miraculously, Lim, Harris, and several firefighters survived and were ultimately rescued from the debris. But Sirius wasn't so lucky—the south tower, too, had fallen, burying him under half a million tons of rubble. The following spring, the dog's flag-draped body was carried from the site with a full honor guard. "In my mind," Lim told CNN, "he'll always be a hero."

IN THE WEEKS THAT FOLLOWED, K-9 cops were a constant presence at Ground Zero, searching tenaciously for survivors and the remains of victims amid the wreckage. Appollo, a German shepherd with the New York Police Department, was on the scene shortly after the buildings collapsed. "To get to the rubble, we had to go through almost waist-deep water," recalled his partner, Officer Peter Davis. "All of a

TED S. WARREN/AP/REX/SHUTTERSTOCK

**K-9 Kato and Officer Kirk Boone on duty among crowds on Broadway in New York City. Police dogs like Kato are key to thwarting attacks in crowded areas such as Times Square.**

citibank
BROADWAY
W 38 ST
W 38 ST
SUPER BOWL BOULEVARD
NYPD
POLICE
CANINE
NYPD
4316 13

ANDREA BOOHER/FEMA/GETTY

sudden he disappeared, fell into a hole. Then this big fireball comes up and he comes running out. He was on fire. I brushed off the burning embers, and he went right back to searching." Working 12-hour shifts for days on end, Appollo and his fellow K-9s became national symbols of recovery.

Over the decade and a half since, with the threat of terrorism now a sobering fact of life, police dogs—in particular bomb-sniffers—have become fixtures at major transportation hubs. Of more than 300 breeds of dog, only a select few are recruited for law enforcement, among them German shepherds, golden and Labrador retrievers, Dutch shepherds, and Belgian Malinois. "We use the shepherd and Malinois breeds because they are the masters of all trades," explains Technical Sergeant Douglas J. Colwell, assistant canine unit coordinator for the New York State Police. "They have great drive in all the three aspects we are looking for—in detection, tracking, and patrol. We also have four bloodhounds who are strictly trained for tracking and trailing." Authorities in Britain have increasingly deployed beagles, because of their superior olfactory skills as well as their popularity with the public. "Beagles are delightful and everyone goes, 'Aaah, they're cute,' so it's not intrusive or scary," security expert Bob Ayers, associate fellow at the international-affairs think tank Chatham House, told the BBC. "They are in keeping with the British tradition of policing—nonintrusive and nonthreatening."

MOST POLICE DOGS COME FROM Europe, often the Netherlands, Germany, or the Czech Republic. American law enforcement agencies buy them between the ages of 12 months and 18 months for about $8,000 for an untrained dog to as much as $20,000 for one that has been fully schooled. What makes them particularly suited to police work? Several qualities, including intelligence, aggressiveness, search and retrieval skills, and physical presence.

No characteristic is more crucial than a dog's remarkable sense of smell, which is up to 100,000 times more powerful than a human's. Whereas police might have to comb every inch of a thick woodland or cavernous warehouse to root out perpetrators, drugs, explosives, or other quarry, a trained K-9 can home in like a guided missile. "The highlight for me and most handlers is when we find our first missing child," Colwell adds. In worst-case scenarios, cadaver dogs have been known to detect bodies buried as deep as 12 to 15 feet underground—or in the remains of a collapsed skyscraper. "We each have a unique odor, like fingerprints," explains Deputy Sheriff Jason Moses, who patrols Skagit County, Washington (halfway between Seattle and Vancouver), with his K-9 partner,

JIM WATSON/U.S. NAVY PHOTO/GETTY

Members of California Task Force 8 and their dog Billy, opposite, searched through the rubble of the World Trade Center after the September 11 terrorist attack in New York City. This page: A rescue dog was lifted out of the pit.

Espo, a German shepherd. "The dogs can pick up that odor. They're so precise in their noses—whereas you might smell a pizza, Espo detects oregano, cheese, and tomato paste and all the other ingredients."

The digital age has ushered in a new K-9 specialty—electronics dogs, trained to sniff out the faint scent of a certain chemical found in USB thumb drives, memory sticks, SD cards, and other storage systems that could hold illicit material. In July 2015, FBI and other law enforcement officials descended on a small suburban house in Indiana and unleashed a black Lab named Bear, who had spent eight months training to detect external computer storage. After nosing all around the premises, Bear froze in front of a hidden thumb drive—the contents of which eventually helped convict ex–Subway restaurant spokesman Jared Fogle, who was sentenced to more than 15 years in prison for possession of child pornography and sexual conduct with minors. "You think about investigators going into a house and trying to find a microSD card that is as big as a fingernail," Bear's trainer, Todd Jordan, told Fox59 TV news in Indianapolis. "It will take [them] hours, especially if someone is trying to hide it."

POLICE DOGS HAVE INDEED COME A long way since their first appearance in the historical record—they've been traced back as far as the 14th century in Saint-Malo, France, where guard dogs helped patrol the docks. The real precursors of modern K-9s were Barnaby and Burgho, two bloodhounds used by London's Metropolitan Police Force in 1888 during its investigation into the murder of five women in the city's Whitechapel district—better known as the Jack the Ripper case. Police in Ghent, Belgium, at the turn of the 20th century were the first to formally train dogs for law enforcement, and over ensuing years other countries began to follow suit. By 1910, Germany had police dogs in more than 600 cities.

In the United States, police used fierce and aggressive Doberman pinschers and German shepherds primarily to attack. Some of the most enduring—and horrific—images from the 1960s civil rights movement show police dogs biting and mauling peaceful black protesters in Birmingham, Alabama. These animals weren't specially trained to obey commands and often couldn't be called off verbally and had to be physically yanked away midbite. "The problem with these dogs was you never know when they were going to turn on you," Mitchell, Indiana, police chief Mike Johnson, president of the American Police Canine Association, told *Police* magazine.

By the 1970s, however, police departments around the country began to adopt a more nuanced and sophisticated approach toward dog deployment. Pioneered by the Baltimore Police Department, which had one of the largest canine units in the United States, the technique now known as the Baltimore Method stresses that dogs should be sociable and at ease interacting with people. The point is that the sight of a police dog should be reassuring, not menacing, to the law-abiding public, whether the animal is patrolling an airport or a crowded city street, or visiting an elementary school.

Whereas police once kept their dogs in kennels, under the Baltimore Method they live together, forging a close bond. "Espo is with me 24 hours a day, which is pretty standard for most K-9 programs," says Moses. "He's basically like a family pet when he comes home—I've got another dog and he plays with it. When we get off work and we get home, he gets fed right away, and he sleeps right next to the bed."

Even during downtime, though, Espo never forgets he's a cop. "When we come home, the first thing he does is smell the perimeter—it's almost like he's doing a security check. I can't go to the garage without him checking it first. When I go to the bathroom, he stays outside the door."

SANDY HUFFAKER/CORBIS/GETTY

**Beagles, like these San Diego County search and rescue dogs, work differently from typical K-9s. Since they're smaller, beagles can be lifted into hard-to-reach areas.**

FOR ALL THEIR NATURAL INSTINCTS and abilities, not every K-9 candidate is ideally suited to the job. Having an even temperament is essential for dog and handler alike, Moses says, yet "you also need someone who's aggressive, a go-getter." Some dogs may possess disqualifying quirks. Sensitivity to loud sounds, for instance, would be an obvious handicap when you'll likely hear sirens and possibly gunfire in the course of a workday. Other dogs balk at walking on certain surfaces—say, smooth tiles or jagged, rocky terrain. Like raw military recruits, K-9s must submit to lengthy and rigorous obedience and agility training. Dogs navigate obstacle courses, learn to respond to simple commands (typically one word), and learn to recognize specific scents.

How do police teach a dog to sniff out drugs, explosive components, and other odors? Often by associating them with a favorite toy—perhaps a simple towel used in games of tug-of-war. The officer will roll up, say, a bag of marijuana in the towel, and in time his dog will link the two scents. So when the animal tracks a stash of marijuana, it's actually trying to root out the toy. "Training is reward based," notes Colwell. "Canines are rewarded

CHRIS MADDALONI/CQ ROLL CALL/GETTY

PETERÁSTEFFEN/EPA/REX/SHUTTERSTOCK

by play, which is an important bonding time between handler and dog."

The length of the basic training varies by state, and it's a continuing education process. "Washington has a 400-hour minimum for accreditation, plus I go weekly for maintenance training," Moses says. "We're a straight tracking team trained on human scent, and we do a three-block track over both hard surfaces and vegetation. We also conduct article searches, in which the dog needs to pick up some kind of evidence along the way, say a shirt or toy gun, as well as building searches, where we'll have a house we hide someone in, or an open area search. One of the more difficult aspects of our accreditation is the 'call-off'—you have to call the dog back before making physical contact with the quarry. If you make contact with the decoy it's an automatic fail in Washington State."

As with most police, a K-9's workday involves routine patrols on foot or in squad cars, and long hours of tedium—interrupted by bursts of activity. Moses, for example, generally backs up other officers who are on a call. If the time comes to cut to the chase, K-9s such as Espo ideally won't make physical contact with their human quarry—but sometimes it's unavoidable. "We never use the word 'attack,'" Moses says. "We call it 'engage the aggressor.' With most dogs it's bite and hold, which means when the dog makes contact he basically holds the suspect, unless the person thrashes around and fights, which usually results in the suspect suffering more injury. Some dogs are bark and hold—for example,

R.J. SANGOSTI/THE DENVER POST/GETTY

U.S. Border Patrol dogs don't bite. In my four years with Espo we've bitten three people and captured probably 100. That's very low on the scale. It's probably because I've just had a really good read on the dog—like in poker Espo has a 'tell,' so when we get closer to the suspect I can feel him pulling harder (he's on a 30-foot leash). His nose is down and if his head suddenly pops up that means we're really close. When I see that, I give a warning that the suspect needs to come out with his hands up or he's going to get bitten by the dog. Usually they give up."

Eventually, Espo, too, will have to give it up—a K-9's career generally ends between ages eight and 11. Espo is five. "We've got between four and five years left," Moses says. "Those are the best years, because we've got the job all figured out." After Espo retires, he'll remain with his partner for the rest of his life. "Handlers get an option, but I don't know too many who have said no," Moses says. "I mean, he's my buddy—he's been watching my back for the last four years, and the bond is so great." ■

**Good police work comes down to good training. Clockwise from opposite, top: Vapor Wake detector dogs are extensively trained to sniff out explosives in crowded environments such as a concert arena or a busy city street; Cobra and his handler, Tom Boskovich, trained at Colorado's West Metro fire station; a new class of tracking hound cubs, descended from medieval hunting dogs, was prepared for training in Hanover, Germany.**

# Celebrity Canines

America knows these dogs on a first-name basis

BOB LANDRY/THE LIFE IMAGES COLLECTION/GETTY

**A Seat at the Table**

**Television star Lassie joined Clark Gable and Ava Gardner at a 1949 dinner celebrating MGM's 25th anniversary in Hollywood.**

**Stars with Snouts**
**Here are two of the most celebrated pups in Hollywood history. Rin Tin Tin, rescued from a battlefield during World War I, starred in movies and gained worldwide fame. After the original Rin Tin Tin died at 14, other German shepherds took over the reigns. Rin Tin Tin IV is seen here with Lee Aker in the 1950s TV show *The Adventures of Rin Tin Tin*. Opposite: Judy Garland as Dorothy holds cairn terrier Terry, a scene-stealer as Toto, in 1939's *The Wizard of Oz*.**

BETTMANN/GETTY

HERBERT DORFMAN/CORBIS/GETTY

BETTMANN/GETTY

SOVFOTO/UIG/GETTY

AHN YOUNG-JOON/AP/REX/SHUTTERSTOCK

**Trailblazers**

**Far left: Sled dog turned hero Balto with sledder Gunnar Kasson in 1925. The Siberian husky delivered crucial antitoxins to Inuit children in Nome, Alaska. Above: The first dog in space, Laika, prepared for liftoff in 1957 in Russia's Sputnik 2 capsule. Sadly, Laika died a few hours into orbit. Near left: On August 3, 2005, South Korean stem cell researcher Hwang Woo-suk and his team at Seoul National University presented Snuppy, the world's first successfully cloned dog.**

GEORGE SKADDING/LIFE/THE PICTURE COLLECTION

CYNTHIA JOHNSON/THE LIFE IMAGES COLLECTION/GETTY

## Presidential Pooches

**Top: Fala rode with President Franklin D. Roosevelt through Hyde Park, New York, in 1944. Above: Millie went eye to eye with former President George H.W. Bush at their home in Houston. Right: President Barack Obama in the White House with Bo, a gift from Senator Ted Kennedy and his wife, Victoria, to Sasha and Malia Obama. Now out of office, the former First Dog lives with the Obamas in their new Washington, D.C., home.**

PETE SOUZA/THE WHITE HOUSE/GETTY

AF ARCHIVE/ALAMY

EVERETT

WARNER BROS./COURTESY EVERETT

## An Animated Life

**Left: Snoopy and his feathered friend Woodstock hit the road in 1980's *Bon Voyage, Charlie Brown.* Top: Scooby Doo and his best friend, the equally jittery Shaggy, solve mysteries with the rest of their teenage gang. Above: Clifford the Big Red Dog towers larger than a house and gives friends T-Bone, Cleo, and Emily Elizabeth a ride in 2004's *Clifford's Really Big Movie*.**

# Just One More

MARK CASSAR/BARCROFT MEDIA/GETTY

"Dogs have given us their absolute all. We are the center of their universe. We are the focus of their love and faith and trust. They serve us in return for scraps. It is without a doubt the best deal man has ever made."

—ROGER CARAS, *A CELEBRATION OF DOGS*